This book is dedicated to Mrs. Johnson.

Copyright © 2023 Jennifer Jones
All copyright laws and rights reserved. Published in the U.S.A.
For more information, email info@ninjalifehacks.tv
Paperback ISBN: 978-1-63731-858-4   Hardcover ISBN: 978-1-63731-860-7
eBook ISBN: 978-1-63731-859-1

Find the Play Dough on Strike lesson plans at ninjalifehacks.tv

Tucked away in classroom bins,
far off and out of reach,
are tiny pots of yellow that
command attention when teachers teach.

They squeeze our dough in desk holes, so that we cannot be retrieved. They shove us in their socks or hide us up their sleeves.

They throw us in the wrong bins
or use tools on us not made for dough.
They bounce us and are too rough with us.
They don't seem to care, though.

Sometimes they mix our colors together
until our hue turns sludgy brown.
They knead us into ugly blobs
and mold us into a frown.

They smack us on the ground and stomp on us, giggling at the imprints that we make.
No, it's not fun being play dough.
There's only so much we can take!

Well, one day the play dough had enough.
They were sick of being abused.
They wanted to teach the students
the right way they should be used.

The pencils called over paper
with the dough's help they began to write.
They detailed all the naughtiness
that made the play dough feel they had to fight.

We DEMAND to be returned to our pots by the color of our lids.

Don't act like you don't know what we're talking about, like you don't know what you did!

You will no longer stomp on us
or stick us in tiny cracks.
From now on you will play with us,
and then immediately put us back!

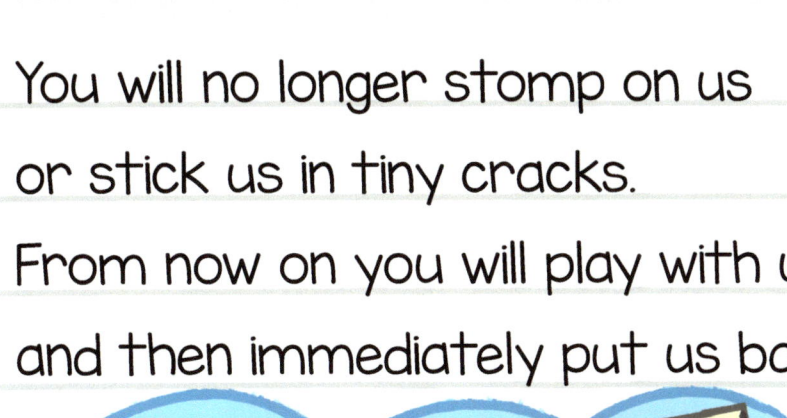

These are the terms we stand by.
Consider them if you'd like.
But until you agree to what we've asked,
we, the play dough, are going on STRIKE!

The students returned to their classroom
to what is normally play dough time,
but their favorite dough was missing!
Were they stolen? Was this a crime?

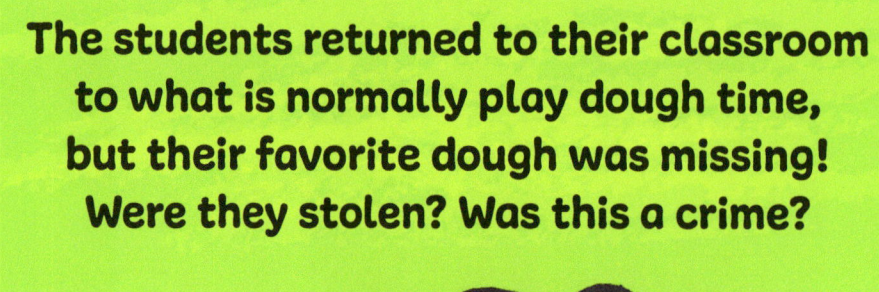

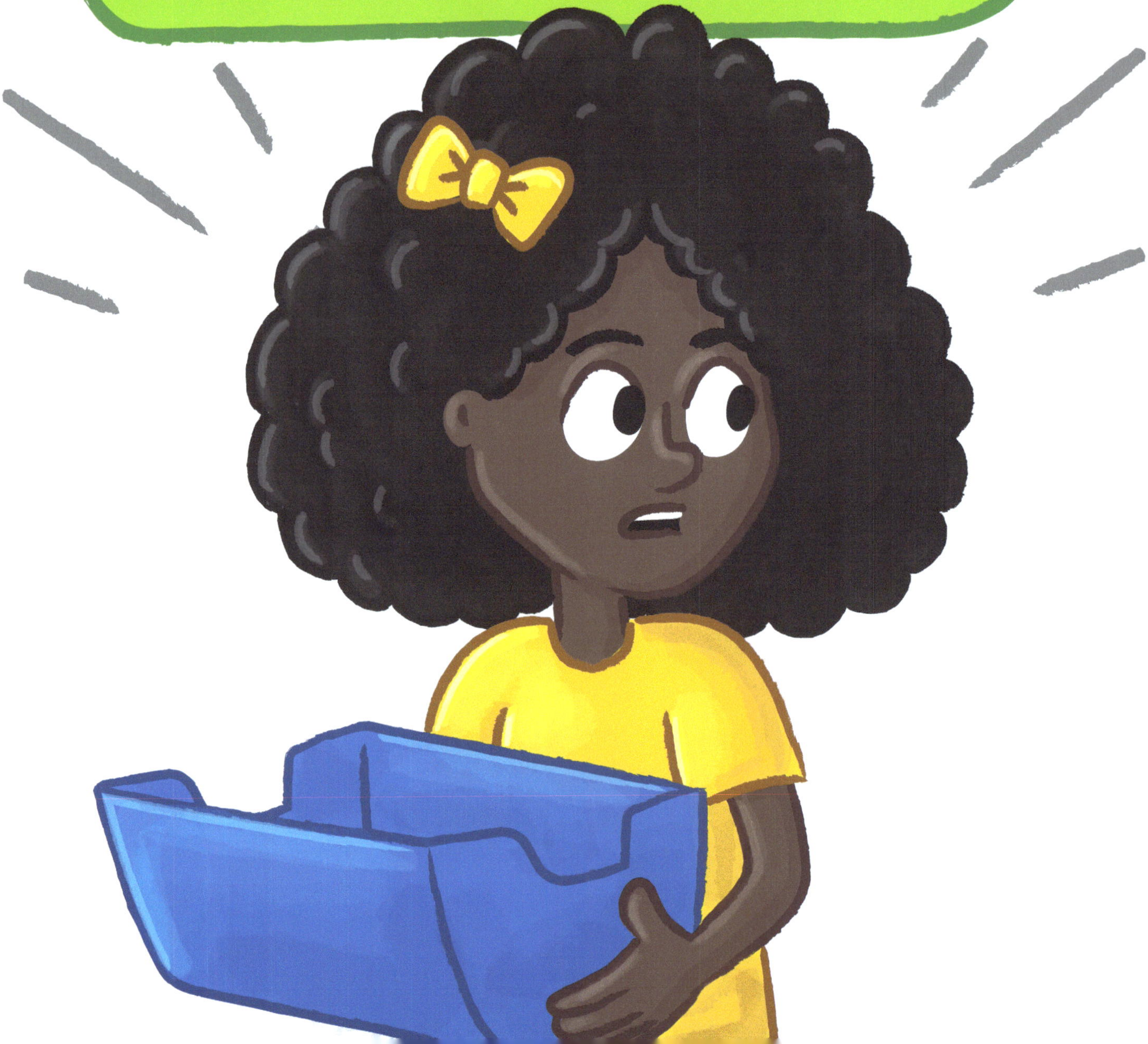

Then one student found the note
and read it to the class.
The students could tell the play dough was angry
and not just full of sass.

Suddenly, sadness washed over the students.
They wanted their play dough to return.
Even though it's a toy,
building with play dough helps them learn!

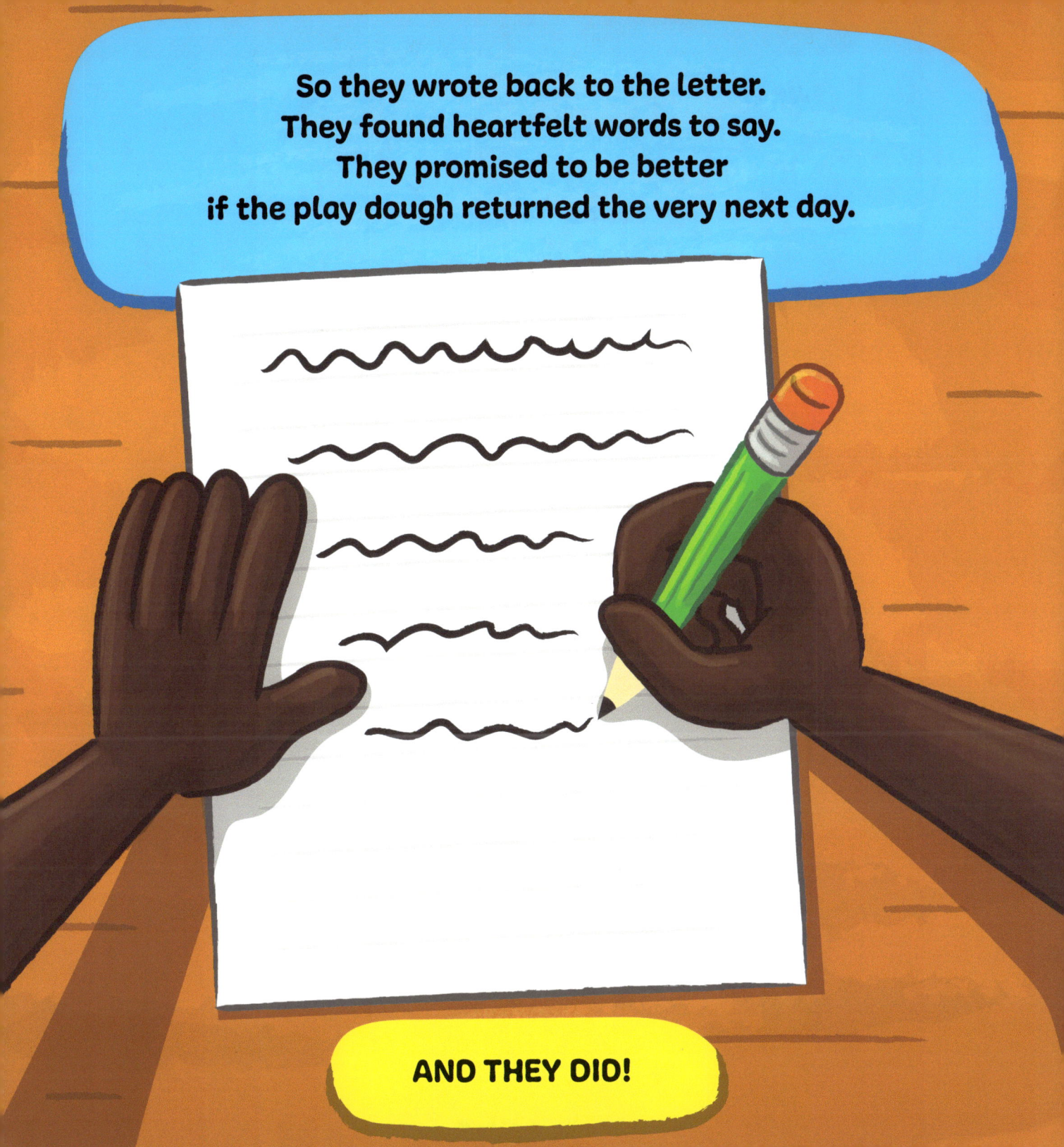

So they wrote back to the letter.
They found heartfelt words to say.
They promised to be better
if the play dough returned the very next day.

AND THEY DID!

www.ingramcontent.com/pod-product-compliance
Lightning Source LLC
Chambersburg PA
CBHW041714160426
43209CB00018B/1829